D1034351

DATE DUE

DISCOVERING WORLD CULTURES

Crabtree Publishing Company

PMB 16A, 350 Fifth Avenue
Suite 3308
New York, NY 10118

612 Welland Avenue
St. Catharines, Ontario
L2M 5V6

Created by McRae Books Srl
© McRae Books Srl 2001

Cataloging in Publication Data

Morris, Neil, 1946-
    Music and dance / text by Neil Morris ; illustrations by
Antonella Pastorelli, Ivan Stalio, Paola Ravaglia.
        p. cm. -- (Discovering world cultures)
    ISBN 0-7787-0239-1 (RLB) -- ISBN 0-7787-0249-9 (pbk.)
    1. Music--History and criticism--Juvenile literature. 2. Dance-
-Juvenile literature. [1. Music. 2. Dance.] I. Pastorelli,
Antonella, ill. II. Stalio, Ivan, ill. III. Ravaglia, Paola, ill. IV.
Title. V. Series.
        ML3928 .M25 2001
        780'.9--dc21

                                            00-069354
                                            LC

Co-ordinating Editor: Ellen Rodger
Project Editor: Lisa Gurusinghe
Production Co-ordinator: Rosie Gowsell

McRae Books Srl
Editors: Holly Willis, Anne McRae
Illustrations: Lorenzo Cecchi, Gian Paolo Faleschini, Antonella Pastorelli, Paola Ravaglia,
Studio Stalio (Alessandro Cantucci, Fabiano Fabbrucci, Andrea Morandi, Ivan Stalio)
Design: Marco Nardi, Adriano Nardi, Laura Ottina

Color separations: Litocolor, Florence, Italy
1234567890   Printed and bound in Italy by Nuova G.E.P.   0987654321

MUSIC
and
DANCE

Text by Neil Morris

Illustrations by Gian paolo Faleschini, Antonella Pastorelli,
Paola Ravaglia, Studio Stalio

🌳 **Crabtree**
www.crabtreebooks.com

List of Contents

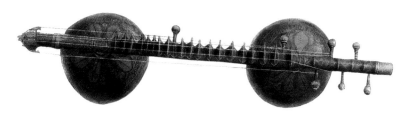

Music

People play and listen to music all over the world. Many learn to play a musical instrument, often just for fun. Others enjoy listening to their favorite songs and melodies. As well as being entertaining, music helps people to communicate with each other. It has been used in rituals and religious ceremonies since ancient times. Over the centuries people have found ways to write and record music, so that they could listen to it on gramophones and then CD-players. Today, music forms an important part of most people's lives.

Tells a story

People have traditionally used songs and music to tell stories. In Australia, many Aboriginal songs pass on ancient beliefs of how the Earth was created.

An Aboriginal songman is accompanied by a long wind instrument called a didgeridoo. This is made from a eucalyptus branch hollowed out by termites.

Communicates

Throughout history people have used music to send messages. Special sounds can act as signals, just as bells are still rung today to call people to church. Drumbeats especially carry a long way. Some African drums have cords attached to their playing skins, and these can be squeezed to make different sounds. Expert players can make these "talking drums" produce sounds similar to their own spoken language.

This drummer from East Africa is using his hands to communicate through the beats of the drum.

An Ashanti man from West Africa is beating out a message with two special shaped drumsticks.

The French national anthem, called La Marseillaise, *was written in 1792 as a marching song. Revolutionary soldiers from Marseilles took it up.*

As big business

Popular music is a big industry worldwide. Pop stars are huge celebrities among young people and influence modern style and fashion. Hit CDs that make it to the top of the charts sell millions of copies and make a lot of money for people involved in the music industry. Live concerts and music festivals are also popular.

Michael Jackson became famous in a family group called the Jackson Five. He became a solo star in the 1980s.

MARCHE DES MARSEILLOIS

Unites

Music is often used as a way of uniting people because it appeals to their emotions. Those who belong to the same nation, or who follow the same religion or cause, feel moved when they hear and sing their special song.

This major scale starts on the first, lowest note called C. The eighth highest note is also a version of C, but an octave higher. An octave is an interval of eight notes.

Is made up of notes

Music is made up of many musical sounds, called notes. The pitch of a note depends on how high or low it is. A tin whistle makes high-pitched sounds, while a big drum has a low pitch. Notes can be arranged in a series called a scale, from the lowest pitch to the highest and back again. There are many different kinds of scales. In a major or a minor scale, notes rise in pitch until the eighth sounds the same as the first, but higher.

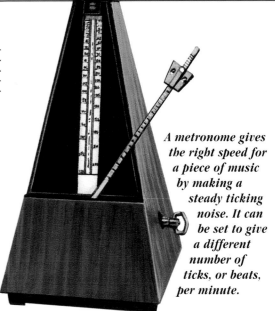

A metronome gives the right speed for a piece of music by making a steady ticking noise. It can be set to give a different number of ticks, or beats, per minute.

Travels as sound waves

All sounds, including musical notes, are made by things vibrating. When a guitarist plucks a string, it vibrates. When people sing, their voices come from vibrating vocal cords in their throats. The vibrations travel through the air as sound waves. Sounds that reach our ears make the eardrums inside vibrate. Information on the vibrations is sent to our brain, which lets us hear the sounds.

Inside the ear sound waves vibrate the eardrum, which moves tiny bones and a spiral tube. A nerve carries messages from the ears to the brain.

Different musical styles have developed all over the world. This blues singer is singing a kind of African-American music that was based on work songs and spirituals. The blues has influenced other kinds of music, such as jazz.

This Indian snake charmer sways as he plays a high-pitched pipe. He impresses watchers by causing the cobra to rise up. When the snake rises, it is actually responding to the charmer's movements, but the audience enjoys the music too.

A musical score can show different parts for all the singers and musicians involved. This score from the Middle Ages is beautifully illuminated (decorated).

Can be written down

Just as we use letters of the alphabet to write words, musical sounds can be written down using symbols for notes. The notes are written on a set of five lines, called a stave. Low-pitched notes appear near the bottom of the stave, and high notes are near the top. Notes also have different **symbols** according to how long or short they are. A special sign at the beginning of the stave, called a clef, shows the exact pitch of all the notes.

In worship

Dancing can be a very emotional experience, and it is often used to express religious faith. In many parts of the world, especially Africa, Asia, and Australia, some dances are considered to be **sacred**.

This dervish belongs to a Muslim brotherhood. The whirling dervishes spin themselves into a trance in order to come closer to their god.

People dancing

When people dance, they move their bodies in **rhythm**, usually in time to music. Most people dance simply to have fun, using their energy to express themselves through movement. They dance on their own, in pairs, or in larger groups. Some take it more seriously, learning complicated steps and even entering dancing competitions. Professional dancers entertain others with their skills: they may be classical ballet dancers, or actors who dance in musicals. People have danced in different ways throughout history, and new forms of dance appear all the time.

In competition

Many ballroom dancers enjoy the excitement and discipline of dancing in competition. Judges award points for each performance of a particular dance, such as the **waltz** or quickstep. The competitors learn their skills at special dance clubs.

Ice dancing is part of the winter Olympic sport of figure skating. Couples perform a four-minute program to music, based on ballroom dancing.

The tango originated in Buenos Aires, the capital of Argentina, in the late 1800s. At first the dance's fast rhythms and close contact between partners were considered shocking. By the 1920s, it had become popular and fashionable in New York, Paris, and London.

For fun

Dancing for enjoyment became popular during the late **Middle Ages** in Europe. It was a favorite pastime at markets and fairs. By the 1800s there were special dance halls where people met to have fun.

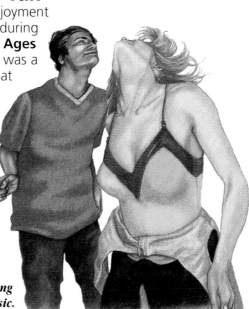

Young people love dancing to the rhythms of pop music.

This painting from 1890 by Henri de Toulouse-Lautrec shows a dancer rehearsing at a famous Parisian dance hall called the Moulin Rouge or "Red Windmill."

The Cossack dancers of Russia and Ukraine are famous for their acrobatic leaps. The higher a dancer jumps, often touching his toes as shown here, the more he is applauded by the audience and respected by the other dancers.

To show skill

Many dances involve a great deal of physical exertion, so the dancers have to be physically fit. Among the Yanomami people of the Amazonian rainforest, different groups perform aggressive dances in order to show their fighting strength. In Papua New Guinea, men traditionally dance for hours at a time and have to be given water and food to keep them going.

In Guatemala, the Quiché people, who are descendants of the Maya, perform a traditional "dance of the conquest." The dance tells the story of how their land was taken by the Spanish conqueror, Pedro de Alvarado, in 1524.

To tell a story

In many cultures it is traditional to use bodily movements and facial expressions as a way of telling a story. **Mime** combines with dance to pass on folk tales or ancient beliefs. Sometimes individual gestures have specific meanings, such as the representation of a strong emotion or a particular god. Modern western ballet and dance also usually tell a story.

A priest of the ancient Japanese Shinto religion performs an imperial court dance from the eighth century. He wears a mask and an embroidered silk robe to portray a prince in battle.

To entertain

Expert dancers can dazzle an audience with their beautiful movements and technical skill. Live performances on stage were popular before the days of film and television. Then, singing and dancing became part of the entertaining plots of popular musicals.

Ballet is a type of theatrical dance, often accompanied by music. Dancers must learn difficult steps that require great effort and practice, but these steps can be designed to create dances of immense beauty and grace. The famous Ballets Russes company (left) led the way in developing modern ballet.

Dancing actors Fred Astaire and Ginger Rogers became famous film stars in the 1930s. They danced together in such popular musicals as Top Hat *and* Shall We Dance?

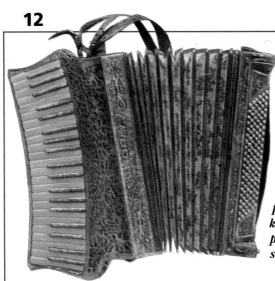

The accordion is a wind instrument that works by squeezing the bellows and pulling them apart again. This pushes air past metal reeds inside the instrument. Its weight is supported by shoulder straps, and the player uses their right hand to play a piano-style keyboard. The left hand presses buttons that make single notes and chords.

This medieval painting was made in Syria. It shows the Angel Gabriel sounding a horn, a type of wind instrument.

Musical instruments

Musical instruments make sounds by causing vibrations, but they do so in different ways. The three main kinds of instruments are the stringed, wind, and **percussion** instruments. Each kind has developed since ancient times, even though their principles remain the same. An ancient harp was quite small and had just a few strings, but the modern concert harp is huge, with 47 strings and 7 foot pedals. Drummers once played simple instruments with their hands. A modern drummer's set is often made up of five different drums, played with drumsticks and a foot pedal, with three different cymbals to add to the effect.

This musician from the Andes mountains of Bolivia is playing the panpipes. The instrument's name comes from Pan, the Greek god of shepherds, who is said to have bound together a bundle of reeds to make music. Panpipe players blow across the end of the pipes to make mellow sounds.

The man in this 16th century painting by Bruegel is playing the bagpipes. He blows into the bag, which he squeezes to force air through the pipes.

Can use air

Wind instruments produce sounds when the air blown into them vibrates. They are hollow tubes with a mouthpiece at one end. The longer the tube, the deeper the note it makes. On many instruments, opening and closing fingerholes changes the pitch of the note. Some instruments, such as the clarinet and the saxophone, have strips of cane or plastic called reeds in their mouthpiece, which vibrate when they are blown.

This girl is playing a modern metal flute. She blows across the blowhole and presses keys to change the notes.

Can be struck or shaken

Most percussion instruments make their sounds when musicians hit them. The most famous examples are drums, which come in many different shapes and sizes. They all have a tightly stretched skin which vibrates when it is hit. One of the largest, the kettledrum, can be tuned to make a definite note. The **xylophone** and **glockenspiel** can also sound different notes, but most percussion instruments, such as the triangle, **maracas,** and most drums, just make one, unpitched sound.

The conga drum was taken to South America centuries ago by African slaves. It is played by hand. The drum is mounted on a stand when the player is standing up. Sitting players hold the drum between their knees.

Hand-held frame drum

The tambourine is a small drum. It has a round frame with a sheep or goat's skin stretched across one side. The metal discs jingle when it is played. You can strike the tambourine with your fingers, hit it against your leg, or shake it. Some musicians use tambourines without a skin.

An Indian woman plays a large, guitar-type instrument called a vina. It is so heavy that she rests one end on the floor.

Can have strings

There are different ways of playing stringed instruments. The guitar and the harp, have strings that are plucked with the player's fingers. Instruments such as the violin and cello are played by stroking their strings with a bow. Another group, including the piano and harpsichord, are played on a keyboard and have their strings hit by hammers or plucked mechanically. In all cases the instruments' strings end up vibrating.

This Irish harp from the 1800s was small enough to be carried around by wandering musicians called minstrels. The harp is over 1,000 years old, and has become a national symbol.

This highly decorated piano was made in London around 1840. Pedals had been added to change the quality of tones.

The body of this 19th-century Portuguese lute is carved in the shape of a fish. The lute is an ancient stringed instrument that was played by the Moors of North Africa. It was very popular in medieval Europe.

In Native American culture, young men who wanted to join a warrior society showed their bravery and skill through daring acts, such as hunting buffalo. They then recited their exploits at public gatherings and took part in the warrior rituals. This Native American rattle was used for a "Buffalo Calling Dance."

In all shapes and sizes

Instruments come in different shapes and sizes, as inventors and craftspeople look for new ways to make the best sounds. Sometimes the results look strange, as makers struggle to make their ideas practical and playable. Many wind instruments are curled up, so that their tubes are long enough to produce low notes, but can still be held by the musician.

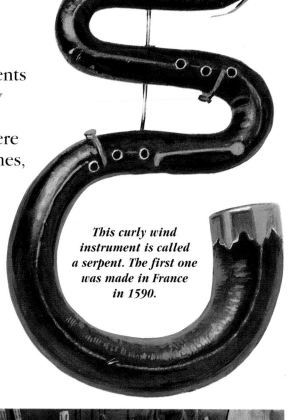

Making instruments

Thousands of years ago people made the first wind instruments from objects they found lying around, such as seashells. They used hollow logs and many other items as early percussion instruments. Harps, **lutes**, and other stringed instruments were made and played in ancient Egypt and China. Since those times, people have devoted themselves to the craft of making instruments that are nice to listen to and to look at. They developed traditional methods that in some cases are still used today.

This curly wind instrument is called a serpent. The first one was made in France in 1590.

Antonio Stradivari (c.1644–1737), the most famous violin maker of all time, studies one of his creations. The Italian craftsman made more than a thousand instruments, including violas and cellos. He used the Latin form of his name, Stradivarius, on their labels.

Using traditional methods

Traditionally, the skills of instrument making were learned over a lifetime. A son or daughter helped in the family workshop as soon as they were old enough, doing simple tasks and learning their trade. Master craftsmen also took on **apprentices**, and in this way skills were passed down the generations. Today, **mass production** has made it hard for traditional craftspeople.

Requires great skill

Even the most talented musicians in the world cannot produce the best sounds without reliable instruments. For centuries, highly skilled instrument makers have carefully learned the craft of working in wood and other materials. The best instruments, such as the famous Stradivarius violins, last for hundreds of years and still sound perfect. Their secret lies in a combination of good materials and expert craftsmanship.

A Polish craftsman is holding one of the many traditional wooden horns that he has made in his workshop. Since fewer people buy hunting horns and similar instruments today, some old skills and techniques are no longer being used.

From found materials

Musical instruments can be made out of almost anything. Natural objects such as reeds or hollow canes can be used as wind instruments. Even discarded factory-made objects can be used, especially as percussion instruments. Most hollow objects make an interesting sound when they are struck with a beater.

Caribbean steel drums are made from old oil drums. The top of each drum is heated and hammered so that the panels make different sounds. The island of Trinidad is famous for its steel bands.

Large conch shells make very good trumpets. This shell has a mouthpiece and is used in Japan by Buddhist monks.

A violin maker carefully varnishes a violin. However beautiful an instrument looks, it is only as good as the sound it makes. Instrument makers are often talented musicians.

That look good

Many instruments are works of art as well as music-makers, and they are prized for their appearance and for their sound. In addition to being well made, they are often beautifully carved, painted, and decorated. Some of the effects are functional too because the layers of varnish applied to a violin affect the way in which the wood vibrates.

This beautiful stringed instrument, called a sesando, comes from Indonesia. It is made of palm leaves sewn together, which reflect the sound made by the wire strings stretched across bamboo. The player plucks the strings with the fingers of both hands.

The back of this South American lute was made from the scaly skin of an armadillo. This animal is now protected and is no longer used in instrument making.

On this 19th-century Indian vina, the bamboo neck is attached to two gourds. Both the neck and the gourds have been beautifully decorated.

African and West Indian followers of voodoo, a term which originally meant "spirit," worship their own god of creation, Mawu. These people dance themselves into a trance when they believe they are possessed by spirits.

Four-armed Shiva Nataraja dancing in a ring of fire.

Religious dancing

People dance as a form of religious celebration. Dancers combine the fun of moving to music with the experience of getting closer to their god. In some **cultures**, dance is used as a way of communicating with **spirits**. Energetic, whirling movements to rhythmic patterns often take the **Muslim** dervish and sufi dancers into a trance-like state. Voodoo dancers also dance themselves into a trance to communicate with their god. In the Hindu religion, the gods themselves dance to show their power and importance.

As the Lord of the Dance

The great Hindu god Shiva, known as the Destroyer, is often shown in the form of Nataraja, the Lord of the Dance. His dancing represents the rhythm of creation, life, and destruction that continually goes on throughout the universe. According to legend, Shiva overcame thousands of non-believers by dancing on the demon of ignorance.

To praise and honor

In many religions and most parts of the world, dance is seen as the perfect way to praise and honor a god or deity. **Hindus** and **Buddhists** use dance as part of their worship. Both religions also have dancing figures in their shrines. The 12th-century Cambodian temple of Angkor Wat, dedicated to the Hindu god Vishnu, has statues of heavenly dancers to entertain the gods.

For the god of death

Many religions have a god or goddess who rules over death, and some use dance as a way of showing the deity's power and influence. Some ceremonies aim to show that death dances among us, since everyone will one day die. Other dances are performed as an offering to a god, so that he will not exercise his power yet, or to try to frighten him away.

A Hindu woman is dancing at a festival in Colombo, the capital of Sri Lanka. As she dances in honor of two gods, Vishnu the Preserver and the local god of Kataragama, she holds a wooden arch over her head.

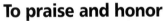

In the Himalayan mountain kingdom of Bhutan, a dance is performed at the start of religious festivals. In the dance, the Lord of Death is played by a Bodhisattva or "Buddha-to-be" who puts off his own salvation until everyone is saved.

This illustration from a 16th-century Persian manuscript shows a Sufi master dancing with his disciples, while others play tambourines and pipes.

In celebration

The physical movement involved in dance generally makes people feel happy. When a group of people dance, they feel close to each other. Dancing lifts the spirits and is an ideal way for people to celebrate their faith together.

A Nubian villager from southern Egypt dances to the beat of drums and tambourines. The dance is in celebration of a Muslim saint's day, and a new dancer replaces a tired one so that the celebration continues.

Can be dangerous

Many **Muslims** traditionally avoid music and dance, in the belief that it is not good to be overexcited. Some Islamic mystical brotherhoods developed their own tradition of repetitive, rhythmic music, and whirling dance. The Sufis danced themselves into a trance in order to forget everything but their god. They often had non-dancing helpers standing by in case they lost their balance.

This man from the Amazon is calling up the spirits.

To communicate with the spirits

In many cultures it is believed that a **shaman** uses his special powers to communicate with the supernatural world of spirits. Dance has traditionally formed a large part of the shaman's ritual. Accompanied by a magic song, dance is used to call up the spirits, heal the sick, and help carry the souls of the dead to the next world.

The colorful Chinese lion, usually with two people inside the costume, dances to the beat of a drum.

The Chinese New Year is celebrated with a dragon dance. A line of dancers make their way through the streets, using long poles to wave the dragon's head and body about.

For good luck

The Chinese believe that dragon and lion dancing parades bring good luck for the future. A festival lion dances through the streets, stopping occasionally to jump up and snatch a lettuce or a red packet hanging from a stick. The packet contains lucky money that was put there so that the givers will receive the lion's blessing and have good fortune. The dancing dragon is also thought to keep away evil spirits.

Choirboys sing in their traditional gowns.

In the choir

Choirs form an important part of Christian worship, by leading the church congregation in singing hymns, or songs of praise. Many choir hymns have been written by famous composers such as Johann Sebastian Bach, who began his own musical career as a choirboy. Young boys make up a large part of church choirs, since their voices are high and clear.

Tibetan monks of the Yellow Hat sect play their horns called rag-dungs.

Religious music

Music is a part of religious worship all over the world. Drums, bells, and gongs are used to call people to worship. Other instruments are played to create the right mood for religious thought and prayer, such as the organ in many **Christian** churches. Music has been specially written for important events, such as weddings and funerals. These events often involve singing, which gives everyone the opportunity to take part in the event. Many famous composers have written music for Christian services, from **hymns**, carols, and spirituals to larger choral works.

In ceremonies

Ceremonial music is important in most religions, including Buddhism. Most people in Tibet practice a form of **Buddhism** known as Lamaism. They see their leader, the Dalai Lama, as Buddha reborn. Traditionally, every Tibetan town has its own monastery, where monks play huge horns during their ceremonies.

At Hindu festivals

Hindu festivals, such as **Holi** and **Diwali**, are accompanied by music and chanting. The sacred **Vedic scriptures** are chanted and devotional songs called bhanjans are sung by everyone. Loud music is played on various instruments, to drown out any unwanted sounds.

These Hindu musicians are taking part in the spring festival of Holi.

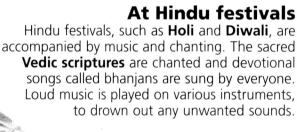

In praise of Krishna

Followers of the Hare Krishna movement worship the Hindu god Krishna. They do so by chanting mantras, or short repeated phrases, based on his name. Dressed in orange robes, Krishna followers play cymbals and drums as they go through the streets to let people know about their movement and to raise funds.

At the beat of a drum

Drums form an important part of most religious music. This metal drum from southern India is played during Hindu ceremonies. It is unusual because it combines five small drums into one instrument.

As a call to repent

At *Rosh Hashanah, the* Jewish New Year, a simple trumpet called a *shofar* is blown. Its sound calls Jewish people to repent and ask God to forgive them for all the wrong things they have done during the year. After that, they have a fresh start on the new year and can hope for good things to come.

The shofar is made from a ram's horn.

For Apollo

The ancient Greek god Apollo was the son of Zeus, king of the gods. Apollo was the god of music and the arts. His symbol is the seven-stringed **lyre**. He was also the god of healing, light, and prophecy. Apollo killed a dragon at Delphi and took over the famous **oracle** there. For this great deed a song of praise and thanksgiving was sung to the god, called a paean.

Apollo with his lyre.

Communicates with the divine

Musical instruments can be used as a way of communicating with divine beings. When priests and worshipers approach Shinto shrines in Japan, they beat a drum or ring a bell. They want the spirits to know that they are there.

A priest beats a large drum at a Shinto shrine in Japan.

Calls to prayer

Various instruments, including the human voice, are used to call worshipers. This Tibetan Buddhist monk (above) is beating a frame drum to call the other monks to prayer. In Islamic **mosques**, a Muslim crier called a muezzin chants his call from the top of a minaret. All over the world, bells are rung to call Christians to church.

Has its own patron saint

Saint Cecilia (right) was a Roman Catholic **martyr** who was killed for her **faith** around 230 A.D. in Rome. Some legends say she invented the organ, which is her emblem. She is known as the patron saint of sacred music for her singing and use of instrumental music in her worship.

Using puppets

Puppet shows have a long tradition. In the past, performances with glove puppets, rod puppets, and marionettes on strings have combined movement and music to enchant children and adults. Music is used to express mood, drama, and action. Puppet characters themselves sometimes play their own instruments.

This character comes from a shadow puppet theater in Java, Indonesia. The puppets are made of leather and wood, and their shadows are made on a screen by puppeteers. Performances of Hindu myths are accompanied by an orchestra of gongs, flutes, and drums.

In the cinema

Film musicals were launched in the United States in 1929 with early sound movies called "talkies" such as *The Broadway Melody* and *Show Boat*. The musical comedy brought a simple, amusing story to life by adding popular songs and dancing. More serious themes were also used for musicals, but the key to their success were the songs. In the original *Show Boat* the hit song was *Ol' Man River*.

Showtime

During the 20th century, music and dance were important entertainment. New musicals, both live on the theater stage and on film at the movies, became popular in cities around the world. Many musicals were put on for several years in large cities. Pop concerts and festivals also attracted huge numbers of fans, and ballet and classical music remained popular.

At war

Movie star and icon, Marilyn Monroe was a beautiful actress of the 1950s and 1960s. She appeared in many Hollywood films and in 1954, she sang on stage for the American troops during the **Korean war**.

Gene Kelly was a popular American actor and singer who appeared in many film musicals. His most famous movie was Singin' in the Rain, *of 1952. The movie was about the change from silent movies to "talkies."*

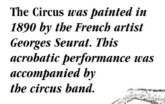

The Circus *was painted in 1890 by the French artist Georges Seurat. This acrobatic performance was accompanied by the circus band.*

At the circus

Music and dance form an important part of any performance at the Big Top. There is usually a large band to play circus marches and introduce the amazing skills and feats of the circus acts. Some clowns play their own music. A famous Swiss clown named Grock, had many musical instruments, but they always had a terrible sound. The only instrument he played beautifully was a tiny violin.

Singing "Feed the world" at a charity concert in England in 1985, Geldof and other singers raised over $72 million.

Many famous stories have been adapted for dance. This ballet is a version of Alice in Wonderland, *by Lewis Carroll.*

For charity

In the 1980s the Irish rock singer Bob Geldof and others began organizing special concerts to raise money to help starving people in Africa. Pop stars appeared in "Live Aid" concerts in Britain and the United States, as well as making a special Christmas record.

At the ballet

Ballet is a kind of theatrical dance set to music. The complete dance usually tells a story, and a **choreographer** decides on the steps and movements made by the dancers. Ballet originated in 16th-century Italy and France, but dancing on the tips of the toes was not introduced until the early 1800s. Some modern ballets have included folk dances and gymnastic movements.

In the open air

In 1969, more than 300,000 young people attended the famous Woodstock outdoor rock festival on farmland fields in upstate New York. They went to see some of the great rock singers and musicians of the time, such as Jimi Hendrix (below), Janis Joplin, The Who, and Crosby, Stills, Nash, and Young. The festival lasted for three days, and the following year a film of the event was released.

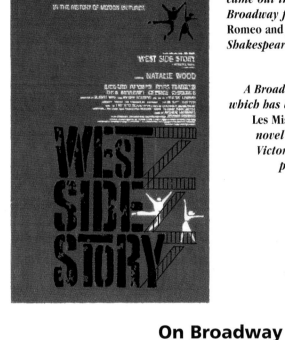

A poster for the film version of West Side Story, *which came out in 1961. The musical became a success on Broadway four years earlier. It updated the love story* Romeo and Juliet *by English playwright William Shakespeare, by moving it to the streets of New York.*

A Broadway billboard for a 1990s musical which has been successful all over the world. Les Misérables *is based on a novel by the French writer Victor Hugo, which was published in 1862.*

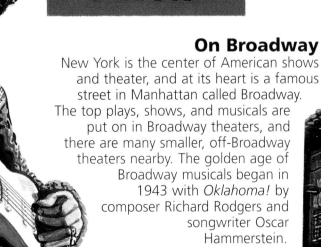

On Broadway

New York is the center of American shows and theater, and at its heart is a famous street in Manhattan called Broadway. The top plays, shows, and musicals are put on in Broadway theaters, and there are many smaller, off-Broadway theaters nearby. The golden age of Broadway musicals began in 1943 with *Oklahoma!* by composer Richard Rodgers and songwriter Oscar Hammerstein.

An orchestra

Most opera music is played by a full **orchestra**. The orchestral music itself is beautiful to listen to. It provides a dramatic background and theme to the action of the opera's characters. A **conductor** stands on a **rostrum** in front of the orchestra, helping the musicians and all the singers keep in time together. They must all work well as a team to give the opera its full effect.

Opera

An opera is a play set to music. This mixture of drama, songs, and orchestral music originated in Italy in the late 1500s. Since then it has attracted the talents of some of the world's greatest composers, including Mozart, Verdi, and Wagner. Opera singers wear costumes, and the stage has scenery and props. The main parts are played by solo singers, who also have to be good actors. A group of additional singers usually form a chorus. Going to the opera is often expensive and is seen by many people as being a special occasion.

A conductor uses a short white stick called a baton to beat time. He also uses facial expressions and body movements to interpret the music to the players.

The Italian composer Giuseppe Verdi (1813–1901) wrote 26 operas, including his famous Aida, *shown (right), being performed in Italy.*

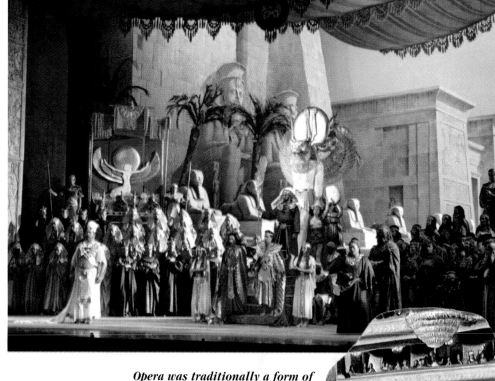

Is created by a composer

A successful opera needs both a good score for the orchestral music and the songs, and a strong libretto. The opera's composer is responsible for both words and music, although the libretto is often based on an existing play or story. The composer must create beautiful, emotional arias, as well as moving the plot along. Often there is a separate librettist: for example, the poet Hugo von Hofmannsthal wrote the words for several operas by the composer Richard Strauss.

Opera was traditionally a form of entertainment enjoyed by the rich and privileged, such as these aristocrats at the Bolshoi Theater in Moscow, Russia. People dressed in their finest clothes and were sometimes more interested in looking at the other people in the audience and hearing gossip than in watching the performance on stage.

Has its first ladies

The main female singer in an opera company is called a prima donna, which is Italian for "first lady." Many star opera singers gain a reputation for being hard to work with and always wanting to be the center of attention. The Greek-American prima donna Maria Callas (1923–77), shown left in the title role of Puccini's *Tosca*, had a brilliant **soprano** voice and was a good actress.

Contains songs

The story of an opera is told entirely by the words sung by the characters, either as dialogue between each other or sung directly to the audience. The words of an opera are known as the *libretto*, which is mainly made up of two types of songs. Arias are songs for a single singer accompanied by the orchestra. Recitatives are used for faster dialogue, and they usually follow the rhythm of speech.

An 18th century Russian opera singer about to give a recital.

Shown in grand buildings

Special theaters have been designed for the world's great opera companies. One of the most famous, La Scala in Milan, opened in 1776. The Royal Opera House in Covent Garden, London, dates from the 1850s. Modern buildings have also been specially designed for opera, such as the Opéra Bastille in Paris and the Sydney Opera House in Australia (right). The roofs of the building beside Sydney Harbor were designed to look like giant sails.

In Southeast Asia

There are many forms of theater in Southeast Asia. They combine music, dance, and drama in a colorful, traditional way. Balinese dancers, such as the masked dancer shown left, act out folk tales based on ancient Hindu myths. On the nearby Indonesian island of Java, dancers move slowly and use their fingers expressively.

A villain and a heroine from the Beijing opera.

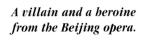

A Japanese kabuki actor in a typical pose.

In China

Opera in the Beijing style is popular throughout China. Plots are based on well-known Chinese stories of the past, and the actors speak, mime, and sing to the music of a small orchestra. They wear colorful costumes, and villains have heavily painted faces. Heroes and heroines have simpler make-up.

In Japan

One of the traditional forms of Japanese drama is called kabuki, which means "art of song and dance." This popular style developed in the 1600s. Kabuki plays are accompanied by music and performed on a wide revolving stage. The actors wear colorful costumes, and all the parts are played by men. Some actors specialize in portraying beautiful young women.

These Hani musicians from southwest China buried their traditional instruments during China's Cultural Revolution of the 1960s. They dug them up again when they felt times were safe.

Culture under threat
Classical culture, including music and dance, is constantly in danger of dying out as traditional ways of life change. Political revolutions, social developments, and religious influences all put pressure on traditional methods. In the 19th century, for example, American missionaries made the female dancers of the Hawaiian islands replace their traditional short hula skirts with longer dresses.

Composers
During the European classical age, composers wrote music that was appreciated by itself. At that time, Austria and Germany produced three of the world's greatest composers: Franz Joseph Haydn, Wolfgang Amadeus Mozart, and Ludwig van Beethoven. Haydn is often called the "father of the symphony." He wrote more than 90 orchestral works.

Beethoven started losing his hearing at the age of 26. He had to stop playing music in public a few years later. He wrote music and finished some of his best work when he turned completely deaf.

Classical
When people talk about "classical music," they usually mean music that is serious and lasting. Classical music is different from "popular music," which is more modern and light-hearted, but is often short-lived. Classical dance, which is generally serious, is based on traditional ways that developed over many centuries. The classical forms of music and dance are not always old-fashioned. They have grace and elegance, and they are brought to life by modern performers. In this way some of the great creations of the past are preserved.

Music in Europe
The period from about 1750 to 1820 is called the classical age in European music. This was a period when works of the highest quality were composed and performed. Earlier music had often gone together with dance and religious ceremonies, but most of the European music of the classical age was enjoyed for the music itself. People began to attend concerts, to listen to chamber music played by small groups of musicians, and **symphonies** played by large orchestras.

Ballet
Classical ballet is based on five positions which were first named in the 1600s. All ballet dancers must learn and practice these positions, as well as many other steps. They must also learn how to dance to orchestral music. One of the most famous composers of ballet music was Peter Ilich Tchaikovsky (1840–93), who wrote the famous ballets *Swan Lake*, *Sleeping Beauty*, and *The Nutcracker*.

Classical ballet dancers, like this one painted by Edgar Degas in 1878, use beautiful movements to express emotion and tell stories.

Costumes

Correct appearance is important in all forms of classical dance, and there is usually a traditional costume for women and men. This may be simple and elegant, such as the traditional ballet dress, or it may be more ornate. In classical Javanese dance, both male and female dancers wear traditional batik clothes, which are dyed by a special process. Jewelry and headgear are usually made of gilded leather.

An orissi dancer displays graceful movements of classical style.

Javanese dancers (above) perform the epic Hindu poem Ramayana *in their traditional costumes. In this story, the hero Rama is the god Vishnu.*

Hawaiian children (below) learning a gourd dance. The dancers must clean, oil and decorate their own gourds before using them in the dance.

Dance in Hawaii

The traditional forms of Hawaiian hula dancing are kept alive by teaching them to young people at summer schools. Hula was originally a religious dance performed in front of the king and people to honor gods and praise chiefs. Dances were accompanied by the music of drums, **ukuleles**, and seed-filled gourds.

In India

In India there is a long tradition of classical dance. Performers often tell a story through a series of movements and gestures. Some forms, such as kathakali dancing of the state of Kerala, tell stories from Hindu mythology. The orissi classical dance of the northeastern state of Orissa, may be 2,000 years old. It is still performed at festivals in special dancing halls attached to temples.

Korean music

Korea's classical traditions were influenced by China. A lot of Korean music is based on a 12-string board zither called a kayagum. This instrument and its music have been kept alive by modern musicians (left). They write the zither music themselves, blending classical and modern music in an interesting way.

Expression of the hands

Classical forms of dance all over the world use movement to express emotions and tell stories. In India and Indonesia the movement of the hands is one of the most important elements of dance. Each type of classical dance has its own language of hand gestures. Classical Cambodian ballet uses 2,000 different gestures in mimed versions of Buddhist and Hindu legends.

This girl needs very flexible joints for learning the special body movements of Cambodian ballet.

These Inuit singers are playing large skin drums to accompany their songs.

Singing

Songs form an important part of tribal rituals. Many of them go along with special dances, while others tell stories and pass on knowledge to the next generation. Some tribal songs are in two parts, with a short melody sung first by the leader and then by the whole group. This is a good way to bring groups of people closer together.

Indigenous peoples

In the past, many **indigenous** people all over the world lived by hunting and gathering their food. Some settled in one place and became farmers. The people in these societies developed their own individual cultures, which included music and dance. In recent times, young people have moved from small settlements and villages to the nearest cities in search of work. Those who want to live a more traditional life keep their culture alive through ceremonies and festivals.

This dancer from Zimbabwe, in southern Africa, belongs to the Shangaan people. His amazing costume includes a mask and a brilliant pair of wings.

Funerals

Some people include music, song, and dance among their funeral rites. The Ashanti people of West Africa believe that a dead person's spirit spends five days climbing a long hill to eternity. During this time mourners fast and sing songs of grief. Other groups, such as the African Dogon people and the Tiwi islanders off the north Australian coast, hold funeral dances.

Instruments

Percussion instruments, especially drums and rattles, are common among indigenous peoples. There are also many wind instruments, such as horns, pipes and flutes, as well as strings. The sansa, or thumb piano, is a traditional African instrument. It is made of a set of metal or cane strips fixed to a wooden board or box. The sansa is played by plucking the strips with the thumbs.

The Dogon of Mali, in West Africa, wear elaborate masks for their funeral dances. The dancers dye their clothing red as a symbol of death.

A human-shaped harp was made by the Ngbaka people of central Africa. It shows great imagination and craftsmanship.

Drums

The steady beat of drums can be heard in most indigenous music. Wooden drums are very simple instruments, but in Africa some are carved in intricate shapes. Sometimes they are seen as sacred objects that are placed at shrines and given offerings of food.

This Ashanti bowl drum from Ghana rests on the shoulders of two carved women. The drum can be used as a fetish and as a musical instrument.

Hunting dances

In the past, hunting was an important part of many indigenous people's lives. In Africa, some peoples developed ritual dances that copied the movements of wild animals. They believed that this gave them control over the animals. The Akan people of Ghana have a special mime dance in which they show how an animal is killed and to honor its spirit.

Flutes

Wind instruments are often closely associated with the spirit world. They produce magic along with their breathy sounds. Many young Native Americans of the Great Plains played the flute to **serenade** girls. The Kamayura people of the Brazilian rainforest believe that spirits live in their long, thin flutes. They worship the instruments in a shrine, bringing them out for special ceremonies.

Tutsi tribesmen of central Africa, perform a ceremonial lion dance after a successful hunt. Their headdresses resemble a lion's mane.

A Kamayura man plays giant flutes, which have spiritual meaning for him. His yellow headdress represents the sun.

Today, Aztec dances are still performed at festivals. These Aztec descendants are dancing in the main square of Mexico City.

Celebrations

People dance in groups to celebrate an event, or to honor gods or spirits. Many dances have strict rules, and young people are taught these rules as they grow up. Among the Aztecs of Mexico, whose empire was destroyed by Spanish **conquerors** in the 1500s, young people were taught dancing and singing by priests. There were dances to the sun and rain, and a bad performance was believed to offend the gods.

Dancing for a good harvest

Ceremonial dances are performed among farming communities to encourage the gods to send rain and for a good harvest. The Native American Hopi people, who traditionally grow crops and raise sheep, have rain dances. Some dancers hold a poisonous snake in their mouth. They believe that the snake will carry a message to the rainmakers, who live underground. In Papua New Guinea, dancers carry grass as a symbol of piercing the eye of the sun to make it weep rain.

This masked dancer from Nepal asks Mother Earth to make the soil fertile.

This Pueblo man from the southwestern U.S., is taking part in a corn dance. He carries a spruce branch and a rattle.

For rain

Many folk customs are connected to the seasons and weather. Farming people usually dance for rain. These folk dancers from Georgia in Eastern Europe are performing a traditional rain dance. The western half of their country has heavy rainfall, while in the eastern half farmers have to **irrigate** their crops.

Children are often encouraged to take part in folk daning. Some, like this boy (right), learn Scottish dances, while others enjoy weaving ribbons around a maypole (facing page).

In tartan

Scottish sword dancers traditionally wear their own tartan, a striped pattern of colors that represents their clan, or family group. The pleated tartan kilts are worn by both men and women. In the Highland sword dance (left), performers jump high over a pair of crossed swords. This young dancer is taking part in a competition at a Highland Games.

Folk music and dancing

People have sung traditional folk songs, played folk music, and enjoyed folk dances in communities everywhere. Many folk music traditions are kept alive today in special festivals rather than in everyday life. Work songs helped people get through long, tough jobs and gave them a sense of togetherness. Dancing helped them celebrate special occasions and have fun. Towards the end of the 20th century, folk traditions traveled around the world and made some singers and musicians famous. North American singers, such as Bob Dylan, Stan Rogers, and Joan Baez, combined traditional songs with modern music in a successful way that is still popular today.

Around the world

In the past, folk musicians and singers traveled a lot. Today, some musicians still travel with their music all around the world. Often their special style becomes a success in other countries. Recently, traditional African and Cuban performers such as Ladysmith Black Mambazo became popular in North America and Europe.

To the fiddle

The fiddle, or violin, is an important solo instrument in many different forms of folk music, especially those that originated in Europe. Folk fiddlers often play fast, rhythmic tunes that are good to dance to. Fiddles go well with other instruments too. A traditional Mexican mariachi band has violins, guitars, and trumpets.

This trio from Madagascar made their own instruments and took their African-Asian style of folk music to Europe and North America in the 1960s.

A Polish musician plays the fiddle in traditional costume.

The cowboys of the grasslands of Argentina, called gauchos, had their own special dances. These are still performed at festivals.

For fun

Most folk dancing is seen as a form of entertainment, giving people the opportunity to have fun together as well as to make new friends. Many of the earliest dances were done in a circle and so linked many people together. One of the most famous is the Sardana dance of the Catalan people in Spain, which has lots of different skips and jumps. It is danced to the music of an eleven-person band.

Around the maypole

The tradition of dancing around the maypole originated in medieval Europe. On May Day, villagers held brightly colored ribbons that streamed from the top of the pole, weaving them around it as they danced. The maypole might originally have been a symbol for the "tree of life," linking earth and heaven. People danced around it to ensure a good harvest later in the year.

This Kalash woman of northern Pakistan is singing at a festival. The Kalash, like the neighboring Nuristani of Afghanistan, have festivals to celebrate spring and fall.

With singers

Many folk songs are sung with little or no musical accompaniment, although there is a lot of clapping and stomping. Young people traditionally learn the songs from older members of the family, often as they watch them work. There are many folk songs about shepherds, blacksmiths, and millers.

At festivals

There are festivals for special occasions and dates. Some are religious and others are traditional. They allow communities to come together. Folk songs and dances tell stories from ancient myths, legends, or sacred writings.

This young Indian woman is acting out one of the forms of the Hindu god, Vishnu. Hindus believe that one day Vishnu will return to earth on a white horse to get rid of all evil.

Drums set the beat for rows of women to sow rice seedlings in a Japanese paddy field. Tunes are also played on pipes.

For working

Work songs developed centuries ago to help make repetitive tasks seem easier and time pass more quickly. African slaves developed a custom of work songs on their American plantations. Many fishermen all over the world sing as they pull in their nets. Drums and other instruments are also used to beat a time for work, and some folk dances have developed from this.

In the desert

People dance for fun wherever they live, even those living in the hot desert. Australian Aborigines put on body paint for their dance festivals called corroborees. The Rajasthani people of the Thar Desert in northern India hold an annual Desert Festival, with camel races as well as dancing. Most desert people, such as the Bedouin of the Sahara and Arabian deserts, begin dancing when the sun goes down and it is not very hot.

The Rashaida people are Muslim Bedouin of Eritrea. Men clap as this Rashaida woman dances.

And romance

Dancing, especially in a pair, is often considered a romantic thing for people to do. In many cultures, the bride and groom take the first dance at their wedding reception as a sign of their union and feelings of togetherness. A person also dances with a spouse or partner to have fun.

Dancing for fun

One of the great things about dancing is that it can be done by any number of people. When people dance for fun, they can also enjoy dancing on their own. They usually find that others quickly want to join in and share the fun. If there are no musicians around, clapping hands and stamping feet can start the beat or rhythm for everyone to follow. Others find it more fun to have organized dances, which have become a big part of special occasions in life, such as weddings, and other holidays and festivals.

All day long

Some traditional dances that tell a story and involve ritual have become part of festivals. May Day became such a festival in medieval Europe. In the Yunnan province of southern China, the Jingpo people hold a special festival once a year. It is called Munao, which means "everybody dances." It starts in the early morning to the sound of pipes, trumpets, and drums. Everyone dances until late at night.

A drummer keeps the beat for the Lahu women's dance.

To reed-pipes

The Lahu people of southwest China celebrate the Spring Festival with an enormous dance party. The best dancers and reed-pipe players are chosen from Lahu villages to perform in front of the **elders.** They reward the best performers with a gift of rice wine. The young women of the villages dance together, followed by the young men. They dance to the beautiful sound of Chinese reed-pipes.

The Munao festival is led by two men wearing hats of peacock feathers. According to Jingpo legend, peacocks led the other birds when they danced in the forest. The young women swing long ribbons as they dance, while the men carry swords.

The Tajiks of the mountains of Tajikistan and northwest China perform an eagle dance to the tune of a flute made of eagle wing bones.

This hula dancer (left) is from Hawaii. Today, the dances are mainly performed at festivals for important visitors and tourists.

In Polynesia

The Pacific islands of Polynesia stretch across a large triangle of ocean, from New Zealand in the south to Hawaii in the north, and Easter Island in the east. The Polynesians are famous for their lively dancing, and the Hawaiian hula is the best known. The hula was originally a religious dance performed by priestesses and warriors. Hula dancers wear grass skirts and flower wreaths on their head and around their neck.

At weddings

Wedding dances are still an enjoyable tradition all over the world. In some cultures, such as among the Himba people of southern Africa, guests dance before the wedding in honor of the marrying couple. The Berbers of northern Africa sing and dance for days in celebration of the bride. In most other cultures, however, dancing forms part of a huge feast that follows the ceremony.

A Himba girl from Namibia dances at a wedding.

In the Roaring Twenties

During the 1920s, people in Europe and North America wanted to forget about the horrors of **World War I.** Young people were determined to enjoy themselves in nightclubs and dance halls. Jazz music was also developing at that time, and there was a series of new dances, such as the Charleston.

New dances of the 1920s were done with or without a partner. So many young men died during World War I (1914–1918) that it was difficult for women to find dancing partners after the war.

American tap-dancers wear costumes to celebrate the Christmas holidays.

At Christmas time

The Christmas holiday has always been a favorite time for dancing. Christmas balls are held in big cities, while people at home have their own fun and games at parties. In Spain, people traditionally dance and sing in the streets after going to midnight Mass on Christmas Eve. In Sweden, a Christmas feast at home finishes with all the guests winding their way through the house in a chain dance.

For broadcasting

The Italian inventor Guglielmo Marconi sent the first radio signal a short distance in 1895. Six years later he transmitted a radio message across the Atlantic from England to Canada. By 1920, North American radio stations were broadcasting music and other programs into people's homes.

An early radio set, which was then called a "wireless." People also bought a wireless kit and put it together themselves.

For playing records

In 1877, the American inventor Thomas Edison produced the world's first phonograph. This device recorded sound on a metal **cylinder** and then played it back again. In 1888, Emile Berliner invented the gramophone, a phonograph that played plastic discs and gave better sound. The original gramophone (below) has a zinc master disk on the turntable. To play the disc, you had to turn it by hand.

Technology

Over the last hundred years technology has changed the way in which music is made and enjoyed. Most of the changes have come through the use of electricity. After people discovered how to record music, they could store and play it whenever they wanted. Early records were large, easily damaged, and had poor sound quality. The compact disks, or CDs of the 21st-century, have a much better sound quality. When radio **broadcasting** started in the 1920s, music became available to all those who were able to afford a "wireless" set. This changed people's attitudes to listening to music at home. The music itself was also developing, and by the 1960s, electric guitars and electronic keyboards were creating new sounds.

This jukebox was a coin-operated phonograph that was very stylish in the 1950s.

It's sheer enjoyment dancing to ~ **Columbia** 'New Process' **RECORDS**

"NEW PROCESS" means NO SCRATCH

For mass production

From the 1920s onwards, records became a very popular form of home entertainment. As record players became more common, the disks themselves were **mass-produced** and sold at a reasonable price. Records were also useful in clubs, dance halls, and at parties, as shown in the advertisement.

Can be fashionable

The design of technical instruments has often made them fashionable. The jukebox was a good example. This special record player became very popular in restaurants and clubs during the 1950s. The jukebox contained a selection of popular records, and by putting a coin in the slot and pressing a button, people were able to play records.

For recording music

Until the 1970s, music was recorded and sold on plastic records. Then tape cassettes became popular, until an important new piece of technology was introduced in the 1980s. The compact disk, or CD, is a plastic disk with a layer of reflective metal. The disk contains a long spiral of tiny pits, which are detected by a **laser beam** in a CD player and converted into sound.

CDs give excellent sound quality and are not easily damaged. In recent years, a new mini-disk version has come out.

In the street

The first Walkman was made in Japan in 1979, and then personal stereos became available in other countries. They were popular with young people because they were completely portable. They could listen to their favorite music while on the move. Older people were not disturbed by music because the listener wore individual headphones.

The personal stereo changed the way young people listened to music.

The electric guitar (right) has a flat body. The knobs beneath the strings can be turned to change the volume and tone of the sounds. This changed the style of guitar-playing.

Electrifies

The first electric guitars were made as early as the 1930s. The modern version of this traditional instrument has a device which picks up the vibrations of the strings and changes them into electrical signals. This device is an amplifier and the vibrations are turned back into loud sounds. Electric guitars were a great hit with pop musicians and rock bands.

Changes keyboards

The first synthesizers were introduced in the 1960s. These electronic instruments make their own electric sound signals that go to an amplifier and loudspeaker, such as an electric guitar. They are usually played on keyboards, and can be linked to computers to change or store the music. Synthesizers can also copy the sounds of musical instruments such as pianos.

On the internet

The development of the **internet** has had a huge impact on many different areas of our lives, including music. It is now possible to visit special websites and download music from them and record it onto mini-disks. This is possible because of MP3, a way of storing music, that makes it easy to send over the internet.

The synthesizer keyboard is played like a piano. Electronic keyboards can be bought for home use.

In ancient Egypt

The Egyptians had percussion instruments such as rattles. By 1500 B.C., they also had string instruments, including harps, lutes, and lyres. Most music was made by professionals for the entertainment of guests. There were also young female dancers who performed at special events.

In ancient Greece

Music was an important part of Greek life. It was played at all public events, feasts, and other social gatherings. There were musical competitions for playing the lyre and the flute. Lyric poetry, which is poetry sung to the lyre, was particularly popular. The flute was usually played at **sacrifices** and funerals.

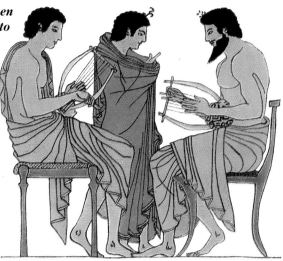

Young Greek men were taught to play the lyre as part of their education.

Music through history

Styles of music have changed since ancient times, but musicians have always influenced each other and certain sounds have remained throughout history. Young women entertained guests with music at ancient Egyptian banquets. Later, Greek youths played lyre music to poetry. **Medieval** minstrels sang about life and love in their day, just as modern rappers tell of life in today's big cities. Some musicians and composers, such as Wolfgang Mozart in eighteenth century Europe, have always stood out from the rest, and their greatness has been an inspiration for others.

This singing minstrel is entertaining guests on a medieval fiddle called a rebec, which was played with a bow.

In medieval Europe

Few people knew how to play a musical instrument during the Middle Ages, but they liked being entertained by others. Minstrels traveled between **courts**, estates and fairs, entertaining guests at banquets and festivals with traditional folk music. Poet musicians called troubadours wrote and sang new songs about love and **chivalry**.

These people are playing music together for their own enjoyment. The keyboard instrument is a virginal, and the other musicians (from left to right) are playing a recorder and a viol.

In the Renaissance

In the 1400s and 1500s, wealthy Europeans began learning how to read music and play musical instruments. They were able to play for their own enjoyment, and they were helped by the spread of printed music sheets and instruction books. Eventually, people were able to enjoy music in their own homes.

To dance to

People have danced to music throughout history, and dancing was common in ancient civilizations. Dancing was popular among the ancient Greeks because they had about 200 names for different dances. In more recent times, special types of dance music have been written for people to enjoy in dance halls and clubs.

This fourteenth century Italian painting shows noblemen and ladies dancing to the beat of the tambourine.

In a string quartet

Chamber music developed in the 1500s when musicians started playing in people's homes. By the 1700s, composers, such as Franz Joseph Haydn and Wolfgang Mozart, were writing chamber music for small groups of musicians. Most were written for the four musicians of a string quartet, but some pieces were written for a **trio**, or a **quintet**. These groups became popular, and chamber music was later played in concert halls.

In the rock 'n' roll era

Rock 'n' roll developed in the 1950s from a mixture of two kinds of popular American music: rhythm and blues and country music. The new sound was a sensation in the United States, and later, the rest of the world. The first big rock 'n' roll hit was a record called *Rock Around the Clock* by Bill Haley and the Comets, which came out in 1955 and eventually sold more than 25 million copies. Rock 'n' roll's biggest star was Elvis Presley, who had his first hit, "Heartbreak Hotel," in 1956.

Elvis Presley (1935–77) made several hit records in the 1950s and 1960s. He also appeared in musical films, and his style influenced many other singers and groups.

A jazz musician plays his saxophone in full flow.

In jazz clubs

Jazz originated in New Orleans at the beginning of the 1900s. It soon spread to other cities, such as New York and Chicago, and then to the rest of the world. The 1920s became known as the "jazz age," and the new rhythms of jazz became very popular. Most jazz musicians were African-Americans, such as the famous trumpeter Louis Armstrong. New forms of modern jazz developed, and they are still popular today.

In the modern city

Inspired at first by Jamaican disk jockeys, rap music developed in the mid-1970s among African-Americans in New York. This type of popular music has a very strong beat, and the words are spoken or chanted in a rhythmic way rather than sung. The style soon spread to other big cities around the world, and top rappers had big hits all over the world.

Rappers Nell Ski (left) and R Rock chanting out their lyrics in 1990.

Glossary

Apprentice: A person who learns a craft or job by working for a skilled person.

Broadcasting: The transmission of music to be listened to on the radio, or programs to be watched on the television.

Buddhism: A religion that follows the teaching of Siddhartha Gautama or Buddha.

Cane: A slender, strong, and flexible branch of plants, such as bamboo.

Ceremonial: Pertaining to a ceremony, often for religious reasons. It includes a special dance, music, and clothes, and is carried out by a group of people.

Chivalry: The combination of qualities, such as courage, generosity, and courtesy instilled in the knights of Medieval times.

Choir: A group of singers who perform choral music, often in a church.

Choreographer: A person who arranges or creates dance steps and then adds them to the accompaniment of music.

Christian: A follower of the teachings of Jesus Christ and the Bible.

Composer: A person who creates and writes music.

conqueror: Someone who acquires territory by force.

Conductor: The person who stands in front of an orchestra or choir and instructs them to play with expression.

Courts: The residence of royalty or large buildings such as mansions.

Culture: The beliefs, traditions, and customs of a society.

cylinder: A solid or hollow shape with two parallel sides and a circular top and bottom.

Diwali: The Hindu festival of lights.

Elder: An older, influential member of a group or community.

Estates: Large farm that is property of the nobility.

Faith: A strong belief in something. To believe in a certain religion and to trust that its God or gods exist.

Folk traditions: Customs, music, dance, stories, and beliefs that have been passed down from generation to generation.

Glockenspiel: A percussion instrument that is made up of a series of bells or pieces of metal layed out like a keyboard.

Holi: A Hindu festival that marks the end of winter. People celebrate it by throwing colored powders on each other.

Hindu: A person who follows the Hindu religion. Hinduism is one of the world's oldest religions.

Hymn: A religious song, usually of praise that is accompanied by a piano or organ.

Indigenous: A group of people who first inhabited a geographic region. People who are native to a region.

Inspiration: something that gives a person the desire and ability to create something special, such as music.

Internet: A network that connects computers all over the world.

Irrigate: To supply land with water by artificial means

Laser beam: A ray of highly amplified visible, ultraviolet light.

Lute: A stringed instrument that is played like a guitar, but is shaped like half a pear.

Lyre: A musical instrument like a small harp, that was used in ancient Greece.

Korean War: The war (1950-1953) of North Korea and South Korea. When the war ended, South Korea gained more territory than it had before the war.

Maracas: A pair of hollow, seed-filled percussion instuments that are held in the hand and shaken.

Martyr: Someone who willingly dies for their religious beliefs.

Mass-produce: To make things, such as clothes and CDs, in large quantities, often using assembly lines in factories.

Medieval: From the Middle Ages. Period of European history between the 5th and 14th centuries.

Middle Ages: The time in European history between the late 5th century to the 14th century.

Mime: The art of portraying a character, mood, idea, or narration by gestures and body movements.

Mosque: A Muslim house of worship.

Muslim: A follower of Islam. Muslims believe in one god, Allah, and follow the teachings of his prophet Mohammed.

Oracle: A shrine where inquiries are made of a certain deity.

Orchestra: Several different types of instruments that people play together as a group. The western style orchestra is called a symphony orchestra.

Percussion: A musical instrument in which the sound is produced by striking a cymbal or drum.

Quintet: A group of five singers or musicians, or a musical composition written for five voices or instruments.

Rhythm: The pattern of long and short beats in a piece of music.

Roman Catholic: A follower of the Christian religion, whose leader is the Pope.

Rostrum: A platform where the conductor stands to direct the orchestra.

Sacred: Something that is holy or worthy of respect.

Sacrifice: The offering of an object, often a plant or animal, to a deity or god.

Serenade: A romantic performance of music people perform to their partner or spouse. It can also be an instrumental composition of music for entertaining.

Shaman: A person who communicates with both the natural and supernatural worlds. One uses magic to cure illness and control spiritual forces.

Soprano: A woman who sings at a high pitch. Also the name of a part in a choir that is made up of high notes and is sung by women or young boys with equally high voices called trebles.

Spirits: A supernatural being, usually thought of as being invisible.

Symbol: Something that represents something else. A printed or written sign.

Symphony: A piece of music written for an orchestra, or the part played by an orchestra in a choral composition.

Trio: A musical group of three people singing or playing instruments.

Ukulele: A small four-stringed guitar from Portugal that became popular in Hawaii.

Vedic Scriptures: The oldest Hindu sacred books.

Waltz: A dance step from Germany that is performed by two people dancing as a couple. The dance follows the repeated rhythm of three regular beats.

World War I: A war (1914-1918) in which Great Britain, France, the Soviet Union, the United States, China, and other allies defeated Germany, Italy, and Japan.

Xylophone: A percussion instrument made up of a series of blocks of wood or metal arranged like a keyboard, that are hit with a hammer. Each block makes a note of a particular pitch.